HIP-HOP HITS

AUDIO ACCESS INCLUDED

PLAYBACK+
Speed · Pitch · Balance · Loop

Audio arrangements by Peter Deneff

To access audio, visit:
www.halleonard.com/mylibrary

Enter Code
5706-3032-3324-1983

ISBN 978-1-5400-8267-1

Visit Hal Leonard Online at
www.halleonard.com

Contact us:
Hal Leonard
7777 West Bluemound Road
Milwaukee, WI 53213
Email: info@halleonard.com

In Europe, contact:
Hal Leonard Europe Limited
42 Wigmore Street
Marylebone, London, W1U 2RN
Email: info@halleonardeurope.com

In Australia, contact:
Hal Leonard Australia Pty. Ltd.
4 Lentara Court
Cheltenham, Victoria, 3192 Australia
Email: info@halleonard.com.au

CONTENTS

BANG BANG
(Rap Version)

CELLO

Words and Music by ONIKA MARAJ,
MAX MARTIN, SAVAN KOTECHA
and RICKARD GÖRANSSON

TALK

CELLO

Words and Music by KHALID ROBINSON,
GUY LAWRENCE and HOWARD LAWRENCE

R&B Ballad

Synth

GOODBYES

Cello

Words and Music by AUSTIN POST,
BRIAN LEE, LOUIS BELL,
WILLIAM WALSH, JEFFREY LAMAR WILLIAMS,
VAL BLAVATNIK and JESSIE LAUREN FOUTZ

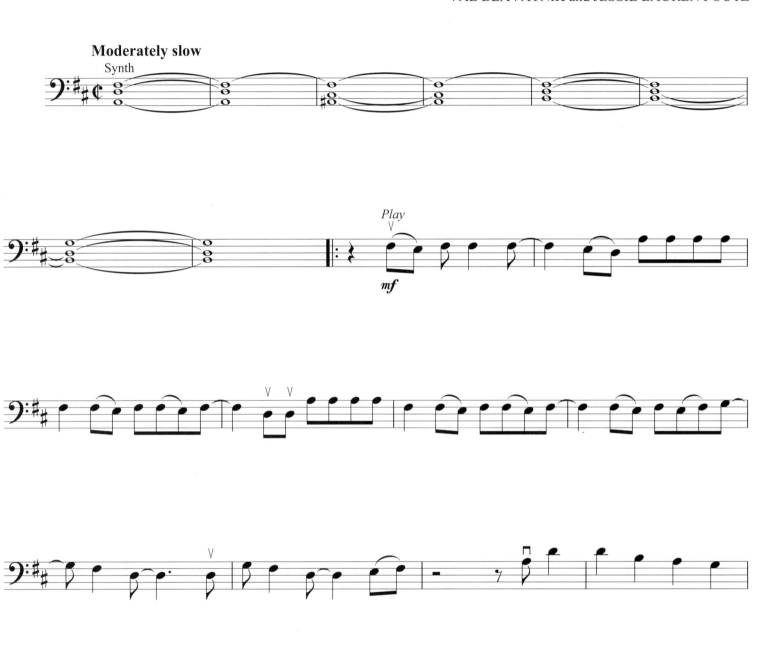

HOLD UP

CELLO

Words and Music by BEYONCÉ KNOWLES,
UZOECHI EMENIKE, DEANDRE WAY, DOC POMUS,
MORT SHUMAN, SEAN RHODEN, KAREN ORZOLEK,
NICHOLAS ZINNER, BRIAN CHASE, KELVIN McCONNELL,
ANTONIO RANDOLPH, EMILE HAYNIE, THOMAS PENTZ,
JOSHUA TILLMAN and EZRA KOENIG

JUICE

CELLO

Words and Music by LIZZO,
THERON MAKIEL THOMAS, ERIC FREDERIC,
SAM SUMSER and SEAN SMALL

To Coda ⊕

D.S. al Coda

CODA ⊕

LET YOU DOWN

CELLO

Words and Music by TOMMEE PROFITT
and NATE FEUERSTEIN

LUCID DREAMS

CELLO

Words and Music by JARAD HIGGINS,
DOMINIC MILLER, GORDON SUMNER,
DANNY SNODGRASS JR. and NICHOLAS MIRA

OLD TOWN ROAD

(Remix)

Cello

Words and Music by TRENT REZNOR,
BILLY RAY CYRUS, JOCELYN DONALD,
ATTICUS ROSS, KIOWA ROUKEMA
and MONTERO LAMAR HILL

SUCKER FOR PAIN

Cello

Words and Music by ALEX GRANT, WAYNE SERMON,
DANIEL REYNOLDS, BENJAMIN McKEE, DANIEL PLATZMAN,
DWAYNE CARTER, ROBERT HALL, CAMERON THOMAZ,
TYRONE WILLIAMS GRIFFIN JR. and SAM HARRIS

SUNFLOWER

from SPIDER-MAN: INTO THE SPIDER-VERSE

Cello

Words and Music by AUSTIN RICHARD POST,
CARL AUSTIN ROSEN, KHALIF BROWN,
CARTER LANG, LOUIS BELL
and BILLY WALSH

WORK

CELLO

Words and Music by ROBYN FENTY,
JAHRON BRATHWAITE, ALLEN RITTER,
AUBREY GRAHAM, MATTHEW SAMUELS,
MONTE S. MOIR and RICHARD STEPHENSON

TRUTH HURTS

CELLO

Words and Music by LIZZO,
ERIC FREDERIC, JESSE ST. JOHN GELLER
and STEVEN CHEUNG